Penguin Education Special

W9-DAV-936

Summerhill USA

Richard E. Bull

SUMMERHILL USA

Penguin Books Inc., Baltimore, Maryland

Penguin Books Inc., 7110 Ambassador Road,
Baltimore, Maryland 21207 U.S.A.

SBN 14 080300 9

Library of Congress Card No. 70-137824

Printed in the United States of America by
Vinmar Lithographing Company by
Vintone Gravure Process

Set in Helvetica

Designed by F. Michael Morris

Photographs for pages 63 & 83 are by Neal Spector.

Contributors

Mel Snyder, Director, Celeste School
Ed Maritz, Director, Los Angeles Free School
Phyllis Fleishman, Director, Play Mountain Place
Herb Snitzer, Director, Lewis-Wadhams School
Grace Paschall, Teacher, Celeste School
Carol Obling, Teacher, Santa Fe Community School
Bob Minkoff, Teacher, Santa Fe Community School
Charles Bently, Teacher, Santa Fe Community School
Margaret Torn, Student, Los Angeles Free School
Cortland Smith, Director, Minnesota Summerhill
  Community School
Vera Williams, Teacher, Collaberg School

Philosophy

Mel Snyder A free school is not a place where you can run roughshod over other people. It's a place that minimizes the authoritarian elements and maximizes the development of community and really caring about the other people. Doing this is a pretty tricky business.

Basically, the best environment is one that has the maximum amount of freedom, the only restrictions being those that involve safety and respect for property and respect for people. In lots of ways, this is kind of an extension of what happens with infants ... it's the philosophy of parents toward their children up to school age. That's the way kids learn how to talk and how to walk, and they're allowed to follow their own natural curiosity all of these first five years.

Ed Maritz A free school is a place where there are a whole lot of things happening. The kids can come and make a choice among the things that are happening, or make the choice not to participate. Kids can work with their hands or work with their minds, or work with a combination of the two. What we try to do is to show that, despite the bad experiences kids have had in public schools, there's a real value in intellectuality. It is one of the many things that is very interesting and exciting and fulfilling to people, not that it has some supervalue that makes it somehow superior to everything else. It's simply fun to learn about the world and to think about it, to analyze it, and to understand things. We try to do the same thing in every other area — art, science, or any activity you like. That's the kind of atmosphere we like to have, think we have, and have had for a couple of years.

People should feel good about what they do every day. They have to learn to tap their own fantasy lives, to learn to get along well with other people. In other words, learn how to build a community based on love and human values, and based on a sharing of the earth, the plants and animals, with other people. I keep the school going because it's fulfilling for me. It's an agency of social change in the sense that the heart of the school is the idea that we could learn to live together, and that we can learn to grow up together — children and adults. We can learn to solve our problems together as people. So I hope a large number of schools are going to pick up from where we are and go a lot farther, and do a lot of better things for people involved in those schools. So far, this school has been changing and evolving continually, and I hope that's always the case.

Phyllis Fleishman Our school just sort of grew the way it grew and I read Summerhill along the way. We became more free gradually. Lots of things that we did in the beginning we just don't do any more, because it seemed that the kids didn't want it or need it. So we just got freer and freer. You know, there are people who expect nursery schools to be decent and free and not regimented. They weren't shocked when little children could be free, but it's still shocking that kids can be free when they start to get older. So, the longer the students stayed here and stayed free, the more free the school was by comparison.

With Sputnik, public school curriculum was just shoved downward bodily. Even decent nursery school-training places just started making nursery-age children behave the way they were going to have to behave in public school. That was directly opposed to the way we were all trained — starting where a child is and going at his own speed, letting him live this year as the best preparation for the next year. They said: 'He'll just have to start practicing what he'll have to do in public school,' and they regimented the nursery school. It's shocking. It just kept getting worse and worse.

I think the whole business about free schools having to be full of love is just nonsense. It should be full of regard for each other. But it just can't be all loving because human beings have all kinds of feelings, including love. We try to have an environment where hostility is an acceptable emotion. We try to have things available and everywhere handy for expressing hostility safely. Tearing newspapers and kicking and squashing boxes, egg cartons or eggshells, things to throw and things to hit, all the time handy. So we don't have an emphasis on being nice and, since we're not afraid of hostility, we don't have to be afraid of stopping a child. We don't have kids scaring themselves to pieces with their own fantasies of what they're going to do with their hostility.

We can do more than just let the kids be free. Neill says, 'The heart, not the head.' I think we can have both.

Herb Snitzer Most schools manipulate kids. You may say, 'What's wrong with that? If you manipulate for positive ends, that's all right, isn't it?' I would say no. Manipulation is no good on the psychological level because you have the kid doing something for a reason outside himself. For us, here, the kids are functioning and succeeding in relationship to what goes on inside them.

In the long run, this will make for a more stable person — a person who will do things because of something within him, will not always need to be stimulated by outside forces. This need for outside stimulation is why some kids say, 'Gee, I'm bored' or 'I have nothing to do.' You never see this in little children. Little children are never bored . . . they're always doing something. To the degree that creativity has been knocked out of a child . . . to that degree a child will say, 'Gee, I'm bored.'

Classes &
Alternatives

Phyllis Fleishman There's just no such thing as being raised in a vacuum that isn't stimulating. The kids all have an exciting appearance and we think we're pretty exciting people. It's a very stimulating world and kids get things from the newspaper and TV. They hear a lot.

We have a lot of field trips. The kids go wherever they want to go . . . and the trips aren't all educational in the usual sense of the word. I think they've been to every museum thousands of times. They go horseback riding and ice skating and to the beach and swimming at a friend's house. Whatever they want to do, they do. But there are some education-type trips that they want to take. We just try to do whatever comes up.

Grace Paschall The parents of high school kids get concerned about science. Are their kids getting science? Right now they're not. There's absolutely no interest. It's not where they're at right now. They are just interested in themselves. They want to know about themselves and how they're doing with the opposite sex. They're talking a lot about the drug scene and the sex scene and that's it. Pushing all this other stuff just wouldn't go. But when they do hit something, they hit if for three months solid. They absorb it, then they go to something else.

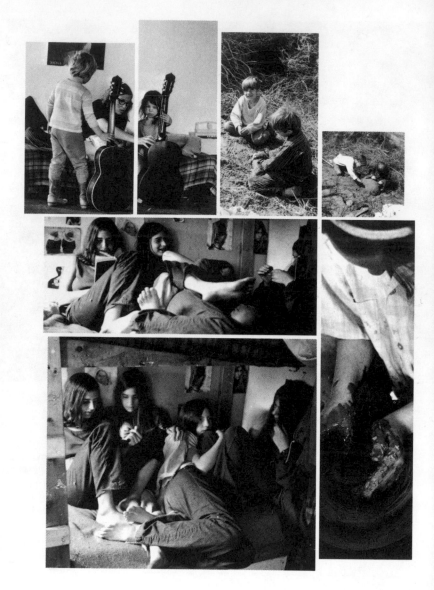

Mel Snyder I think there are times when all the parents who send their children here wonder: 'Are my children going to be able to get into college . . . are they going to be able to go through another high school, if they change their minds about this form of education? Are the kids going to get 'turned on' to all the things that a lot of adults find are exciting in areas of science and mathematics, when no one's pushing them to develop in these areas?' I don't know . . . they may not. It involves a kind of faith that even says 'Well, suppose they don't . . . maybe that excitement is my thing, not their thing, so let them come to whatever excitements are theirs.'

I feel that if we can just let ourselves and the kids go totally free with their lives, their awareness, then gradually we and they will learn the essential things to know, which are 'Who am I?' and 'What is my life all about?' But that's a hard thing to do.

Carol Obling If the children want grades, I tell them to give them to themselves. Some of them do, some of them have been in public schools and have pretty concrete concepts as to whether they should get an 'A' for doing this, or a 'B' for doing that, or a 'C' if it's not so good.

The older boys are out on a camping trip. To find themselves motivated to take math and English is a little harder for them. But one of the older boys just took a test to go into a public school here. In the beginning of the year, he was two years behind in his reading. He's supposed to be in the fourth grade, but he was reading at a second-grade level. When he took the test, just a couple days ago, he was only three months behind other fourth-graders.

A Student I like this school better because you can just about do anything you want. The other one I went to was real strict and they made you do things. Here, if they have ballet or something, they don't make you do it . . . you can just do it if you want. I'm glad about that because I don't like ballet.

Sometimes, I go read to the little kids . . . stories and stuff like that . . . then I go in the pottery room and do leather work and stuff like that. In public school, you can't do things like that. You can only do certain things that are scheduled for the day. Here it just happens and you do it.

A Student Teacher I'm learning from the kids as much as they're learning from me. A lot of the kids are brats, but it's really a better way for them to learn.

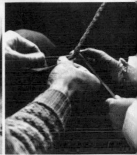

Bob Minkoff Here some of the problems are: How do you get kids to come along and read? How do you get a kid, scared of trying new things, to try it just one time, and get a little success and go on?

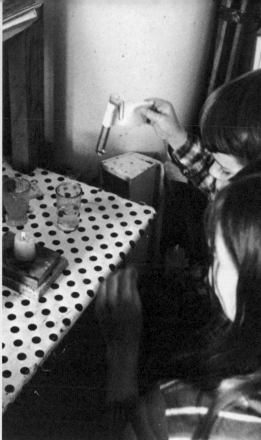

Charles Bently The freedom that the kids have is very appealing. But the problem is how to carry on some degree of traditional learning within the framework of this freedom. What intrigues me most is to lure the kids in, to find approaches that make the subject matter irresistible to the kids, and develop games that lead into significant ideas about what you want them to learn.

In general, we should make it as interesting as possible, so that the frame of freedom doesn't work against the education that we feel — and most people

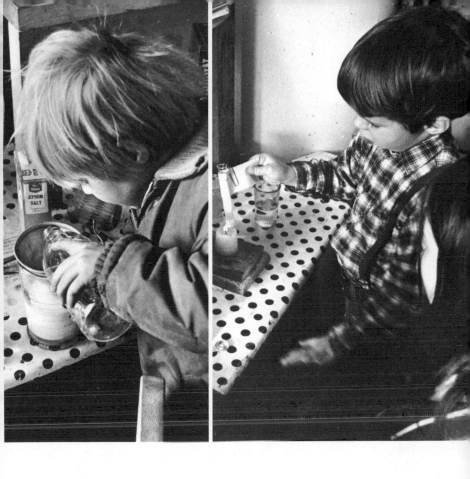

expect — should be going on in school. I think that if a kid at this school knows how to add, he knows a lot more than just pushing symbols around on a piece of paper. It has meaning for him in terms of real objects.

For the last few weeks the kids have been messing around with soda and vinegar. I've been amazed by the way the kids have stayed with it . . . and amazed at the deliberateness of their investigation. I've seen five-and six-year-olds sit down for an entire afternoon, mixing, pouring, and watching what happens.

Margaret Torn When I was in public school, I didn't learn anything
... didn't do anything there that was worth anything
besides some learning.

Ed Maritz We have sixty kids and seven full-time teachers. The
seven full-time teachers, I think, are really fine people.
They are good with the kids. The kids love them and they
love the children. They have a tremendous variety of
different skills and talents. One woman teaches physics,
chemistry, physiology. She plays about twenty different
instruments, and that's not an exaggeration. She writes
music, sings, does all kinds of craft work — silk screen-
ing, and so forth. And she's a typical teacher at this
school. The other teachers have similar wide ranges of
interests and capabilities.

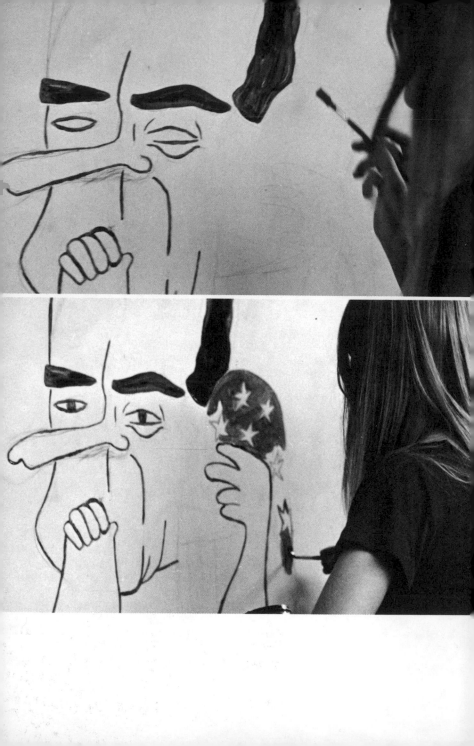

Vera Williams It's not just that it's kinder to the kids to allow them to do what they want; nor can you just say to parents 'so what does it matter it he doesn't learn?' This isn't what turns out to be true. What is true is that that is the way you learn, and you learn by having a vastly expanded environment, by having a lot of variety, a lot of static, a lot of things that distract you. You learn in exactly the opposite way you thought you did.

Cortland Smith At the beginning of each semester, we have a meeting with each kid and we ask him what classes he wants. Then we write down all the ideas they have for classes. Next the staff gets together and decides what they can teach. Someone on the staff then makes up a schedule and we proceed from there. The kids show up and see if they really want the class or not. Usually, in the beginning, the schedule is jampacked. Then, if at least one of the kids doesn't show up for this class — say four or five times — we just drop it and put another one in there. Otherwise, we haven't enough time to do it all.

The small kids mostly want reading and writing and math classes — really their basic interest along with the science class. Actually they want kind of traditional things, so for the most part we have pretty traditional kinds of classes. They last about an hour. The older kids have seminar classes. They meet once or twice a week for three hours at a time. Their scheduling is a little bit different. They may have classes in the afternoon or evening or whatever. Literature classes, math classes, music appreciation, French, kind of traditional things again. We had a psychology class and a general social science class.

Herb Snitzer The usual kind of classroom situations do not exist here. A teacher is not an authority figure. He's not a disciplinarian. He's not a marker of tests. He's not someone to ask permission to leave the room, and all the rest.

Self-Government

Richard Bull This to me was one of the most impressive features of these schools. It is startling to find that a truly democratic form of self-rule not only can work with adults, but with kids as well. The kids themselves handle most of their own problems among themselves. It is a fact that at the best free schools the kids are first and foremost in control of their own lives — visibly and actually in control.

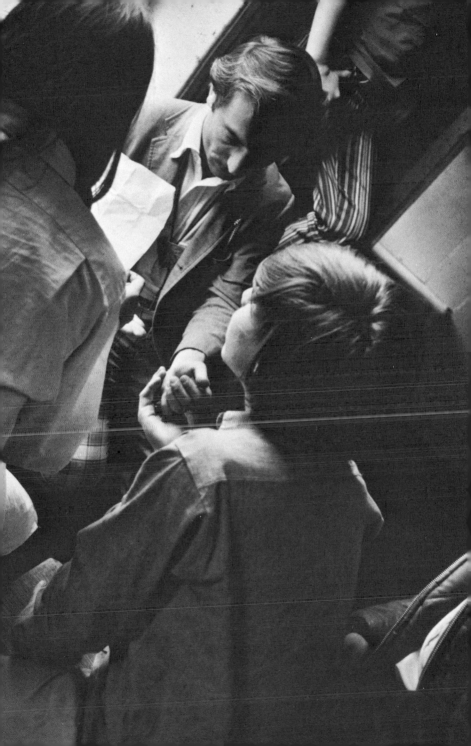

Herb Snitzer The adults have rights on the human level that are just as valid and just as real as any of the kids here. On a political level, you might say: 'No, they don't have equal rights with the kids. Teachers have to show up for classes! Kids don't.' Legality and humanity are not always mutually inclusive.

Margaret Torn The meetings are sometimes adjourned before I can get my things said. And I don't like the things we do, sometimes, like having majority votes. I like consensus: you take the majority vote, then if someone doesn't like it, you work it out so everyone likes it, so everyone's satisfied. With a majority vote, there's always people who get screwed. I don't think that's very fair, if there's a way to help it, and there usually is.

Sometimes, I'm the one who gets screwed. Most of the time I don't, but I still don't think it's very fair.

Ed Maritz If a school is really free-swinging and evolving, and if it's genuinely run by the people involved, that means all the children and all the adults, I think you could then probably handle a couple of hundred kids.

Mel Snyder If there are one or two destructive members of the group, we've found the best way for the school to handle this kind of problem is by letting the kids handle it. It usually works very well to go through the kind of school-meeting process because the majority of kids usually don't like to see destructiveness. And they'll find some way of handling it — either expel the kid or find some appropriate consequence for his behavior.

Cortland Smith The kids have their own rules that they made which are posted in the dome. That includes the quiet at 10:30, and you can't climb on someone else's wall, and you have to knock before you enter a room. Then there are safety rules the staff has made. You can't go swimming unless you go with someone else. You have to tell some-one you're leaving the island if you are leaving. That's so that we know where you are or know that you've disappeared. You can't have any fires on the island except in the fire circle. That's about it.

4

Staff & Parents

Phyllis Fleishman Some free schools just take the kid and disregard the parent, but we feel we must be able to work with the parents in order to do any good. Parents can come here whenever they want. They're encouraged to visit . . . to do and give anything to the school they want.

A very uncomfortable thing is to have an anti-parent attitude which I think Neill certainly had. He just gave

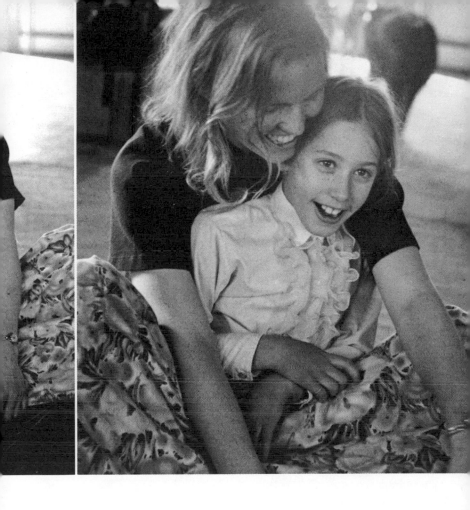

up on them as hopeless. We try here to enter only those who don't seem hopeless, so we can really work with them. And they do seem to change. We have a systematic approach to parents. We have six meetings especially for the new parents, when they come every year. Then we have meetings every month on topics of general interest.

In that vein, the staff meets with a psychologist once a month and I think that's essential. I know that in some other schools the staff just doesn't have a way of working out the things that they have between them. Staff may try to be cool and planned but they need time to work out the things that are uncomfortable for them. I think this is one thing that helps us, now that we're bigger. It helps us to stay healthy.

Carol Obling Paid staff at this point is about twelve or thirteen. But we have a lot of volunteers. Parents volunteer, if they feel they can give something special. We have a lot of Indian and Spanish children here in the school. Some of the Indian parents come in and help with the pottery. Indians don't use a wheel, so the kids learn to pinch and do coil pots.

Charles Bently To me one of the most attractive sides of this school is that anybody can get into the classroom if he's dedicated, if he's willing to put up with the abuse that he might suffer during the first few days it takes the kids to test him and to find out who he is. If he can put up with all that and not be mean with the kids, why he's welcome. Even if he's only coming to play games with the kids, it's great because kids seem to desire genuine relationships with adults. Adults they can trust, be friends with, and call by their first names and horse around and have fun with them.

Herb Snitzer It's very difficult for adults to live here because the role of an adult in this school is not just to be one of the boys. There are very valid functions for adults here. One of them is to function in a way that lets the kids know this is a safe place . . . a stable place . . . that they can act out whatever they need to act out, and they will not be brutalized for it or smacked down physically for what they do. If they do something that is intrusive, they will be called on it. But they will not be hurt, either physically or verbally. There's none of that moralizing that adults are so great at with kids to the point of making them feel pretty guilty. In many ways, an adult has to perform this function of security,

of being a secure element, a stable element. So they have an important job to do — not as teachers, but as human beings.

A teacher cannot slap out in anger. Kids have come up to me and said, 'I'm going to punch you.' And I said, 'Okay, but just understand that if you punch me, I'm going to punch you,' depending on who the kid is. Sometimes I let a kid hit me because he needs to do it. I represent papa to him . . . I represent authority to him, especially if he's a new kid. I know that the process is working on a new kid when he can come up to me and punch me in the arm. That little gesture — hitting the principal of a school — tells me so much about how far that kid has come. And yet there are times when a kid will come up to me and hit me, and I'll just bop him on the arm. But it won't come out of anger or out of hatred or from the attitude: 'I'm going to get back at you because you've done it to me.'

When something happens, an incident of any kind, you've got to be there. Hopefully, more times than not, you're there in a way that will be supportive to the kid. Because if the kid feels that you can't be, then your usefulness, so to speak, in terms of Lewis-Wadhams, becomes minimized.

I think we've created a feeling of stability over the last seven years. Hopefully, other schools will not only exist, but have this kind of stability for kids. There are schools that have existed for years, but every June there's always the question of whether they're going to open in September. And this is no good for kids.

All staff members change, every adult who walks into this place changes. By definition they have to. They come from what I consider a basically oppressive culture into one that is not, so all the defenses, all the ways of living that adults have known, no longer apply.

We have staff workshops for adults at the beginning
of each term. This is where my wife comes in . . . she's
very perceptive. These workshops are revelations for
the new staff people. People now call them sensitivity
training or T groups, but we've been doing this ever
since we've been here. We not only get into the
psychological aspect of the person, but also what
they want to do here as teachers who are going to
be in a particular area with particular kids, covering
particular subject matters. Many adults come here
who can't stand to write. Now how the hell can they
have a kid write it they, as teachers, can't stand
to write?

You know, reading about freedom and experiencing
it on a gut level are two different things. Knowing that
kids swear and hearing them say, 'Fuck you,' are just
two different things. When a parent first hears a kid do
this and do it right on, it's really terrifying. Suddenly,
all the anxieties and apprehension that the parent has
come to the surface. So I spend a lot of time talking
about this kind of thing with parents.

Many parents are confused about freedom themselves. They'll go to a school where there are lots of
drugs, let's say, and they might rationalize by saying,
'Well, that's freedom. If a kid wants to indulge in
drugs, who am I to say no?' This only lets me know
that the parents can't say 'No'.

Mel Snyder One of the main reasons parents send their children to a school like this is because the parents like the adults and respect them as individuals. So it's really important to have that person-to-person contact with parents.

The way we've gotten our staff has been interesting. They've always been people who have come to the school and liked it here very much, rather than people we've recruited. They've just kind of liked the whole way of life. From my point of view, this is a very satisfying method of acquiring staff.

Mel Snyder One of the things I think is unique about our school that most free schools haven't tried, is that we are working without a director. All staff people discuss the issues together. We're really working much more like a family works, with a husband and wife making the decisions without one of them being boss. Only in this case it's five to seven staff members who are doing it. Two of our staff mentioned, when they arrived, that at some free schools they'd visited the hangups of the director were passed right on down the structure of the school. I don't know whether we're getting the hangups of seven people instead of one or are avoiding some of that kind of problem.

Ed Maritz It seems to me that a free school has to have a core of people who see themselves as dedicated teachers, as professionals. But not all teachers are full-time. I'll give you an example. We have a fellow who comes here. He's about sixty-five. He works as a window washer to support himself. He was having trouble — high blood pressure — and he wasn't feeling good. He went to a doctor who told him: 'Well, hell, you're cut off. You're not having any relationships with anybody, you live by yourself. You've got to get out in the world, get to know some people, relate to kids.'

So the man just came by the school. He comes and he sits and talks. He's not an intellectual, he never heard of Summerhill, but he likes children and this is a place where somebody would let him come. He's really a valuable man . . . and he loves kids. His blood pressure is down . . . he's healthier.

Living in Freedom

Mel Snyder The biggest hope I have is that the kids will grow up very integrated with their lives. But I can only picture that to the extent that I have experienced it personally or witnessed it in other people. These people have a strong sense of self and don't need to be swayed by other people's opinions. They're open and they're listeners. Life to them is a constant learning process. There's no final answer.

My oldest girl, now twelve, was very tense when she was in public school. She did well, but she worried about all kinds of things — social acceptance, getting her homework done, things like that. When she's here, she doesn't worry at all because there's nothing to worry about.

Richard E. Bull The "ultimate faith," I'm told, is to be able to say "so what?" if a normal child has not learned to read and write by the time he's twelve or thirteen. In fact, this situation rarely occurs. The students pick up the fundamentals whether they attend formal classes or not.

Richard Bull According to Psychologist Andrew Slater: To build a happy child, parents need be guided by only two precepts.

Give the child a great deal of love. Not "smother" love but a feeling of being appreciated and encouraged. The child who feels loved, accepted by his environment, will be well adjusted.

Don't overprotect the child. Let him learn the hard way, through doing and through experience.

This should guide parents in their selection of a school for their children.

Charles Bently Kids straight out of public school take a while to figure out what to do with their time. 'Gee, I'm not expected to be any place at any time. I'll just wander around for a while.' But after a while, they become very good at using their time. We notice it in the older students. The moment they get to school they're doing something, making choices on what they'd like to do next.

After a teacher's been at a school like this for a while, he begins to see much more of a validity in the hour-to-hour activities of the kids. At first, he'll think they're just wasting their time because they're not doing what he had thought they should be doing that day. But after he's watched them for several weeks — maybe it takes months — he begins to say: 'So-and-so has been spending a lot of time on this or that.' He begins to see the discipline in what the kid's doing. Just because no one has told him to do something doesn't mean the kid isn't disciplined. Actually, he's disciplining himself.

Lots of times we found that kids who had trouble reading were on the outskirts of the reading activities, watching over somebody's shoulder. The kids are really picking up a lot in ways that we don't always notice.

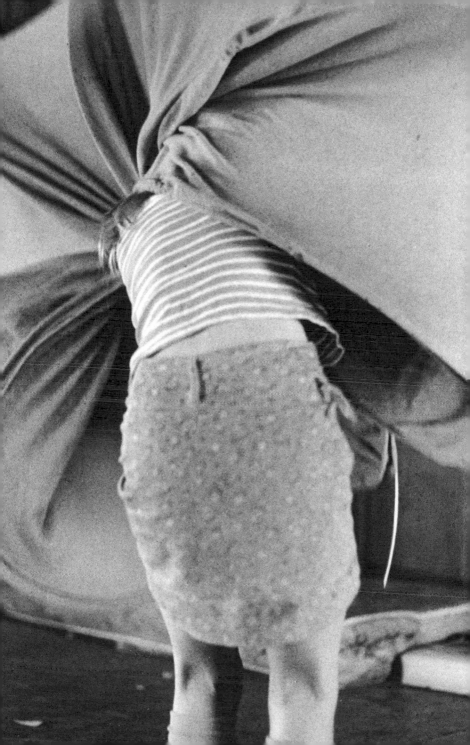

Bob Minkoff

I think that differences in attitudes toward younger and older people are characteristic of these kids as they grow older. They are willing to learn from elders and young-sters, whereas our parents were interested in teaching, in passing it on down.

Obviously, 'hip people' tend to be the majority of people who send their kids to community schools. But all these schools I know have really tried to get black kids, Chicano and Indian kids all for free. These people are our brothers and we try to relate to them. Some-times it's a difficult prob-lem, a cultural problem. A lot of these people have just spent years getting their kids into public school, and they're afraid to take them out of the public school and put them into this 'hippy' school. That is a problem.

Jennifer Snyder At public school you do, and at free schools you do and be.

Phyllis Fleishman The kids who have been here since they were four or five are the ones we're really excited about. They're fabulous. But we've had a couple of those kids who were fantastically 'turned off.' I couldn't believe it. They had to prove that they weren't going to do anything, just nothing. It's a sad thing to see. It's frustrating to me. Eventually, I found the same feeling in me that the parents have. I wanted them to do something, just anything.

We've found that the kids who go from here to public school put up with what they have to put up with. The idea is that if they've had lots of satisfying experiences and if they've learned how to be creative and find ways to do the things they want to do, then they can do them even while they go to public school. For the most part, they're able to handle frustration better than people who haven't been able to express their frustration all along, as our kids can and do.

Cortland Smith We had a kid at sixteen going to the University of Minnesota. Another kid at sixteen went to the Minneapolis School of Arts. One kid at eighteen went to Marlboro College. Another quit here at sixteen and started pumping gas. He did that for about two months, then he came back. He stayed for half a year, then joined the navy.

Basically the situation is that you read the catalogues, and if you agree with what's happening in the school you send your kid here. If you don't agree, you shouldn't send him.

Ed Maritz When I first started the school, my model was that I assumed the kids would go to the school, that they'd become involved in things, get a sense of their own identity. I figured they would reach a point where they were fairly well self-regulated, self-actualized, and they'd leave the school and go out to fairly standard outside occupations. But what really happened is that the kids picked up the dynamics of the school the longer they were here, and some of the kids who have been here for three or four years now have not only really transformed the school, but in the process have transformed me too.

I see now that most of the kids in this school are not going to go into traditional occupations in the sense that I thought they would. Most of them are not going right into college, not because they couldn't but because they don't choose to go. Most of them are so vitally alive that they're starting to create all kinds of new ways of living . . . new concepts of what you can do with your life to make it worthwhile.

One girl who graduated here when she was sixteen has decided that she wants to travel through Europe for a few years and then start a school of her own.

Herb Snitzer These kids have a tremendous amount of tolerance for each other. Say a kid goes up to Fred and hits him. Fred wouldn't go after him. He may want to, but he won't do it because he knows or has come to realize who this kid is, what his needs are to do this type of hitting. And even if Fred wanted to beat the shit out of him, he wouldn't do it because it wouldn't solve anything and Fred knows it.

Some people have the idea that Summerhill or Lewis-Wadhams are places where everybody can do what they want. They're not. But there are schools

that are run like that . . . and I hope they fail. I hope
they fail because I think they hurt kids. I think those
adults have to grow up and understand that it's a
serious thing when you take in your hands the life of
another person, especially a young person . . .
or else get the hell out from behind the Summerhill
idea . . . don't hide behind it. If you want a place
where everybody balls everybody else, fine. But don't
call it Summerhill, don't call it freedom. Call it
infantilism . . . call it sickness . . . call it perversion.
Don't call it freedom . . . don't call it Summerhill
because that has nothing to do with it.

List of Schools Visited

For a more complete list of American Summerhill Schools, contact The Summerhill Society, 339 Lafayette St., N.Y.C. 10012

Celeste School — day and boarding, ages 5 to 12. Celeste School, 422 Camino De Bosque, N.W., Albuquerque, N.M. 87114

Collaberg School — day and boarding, ages 3 to 17. John Carson, Collaberg School, Theill's Rd., Stony Point, N.Y. 10980

Green Valley School — boarding, ages 4 to 21. George Von Hilsheimer, Box 606, Orange City, Fla. 32763. And Buck Brook Farm, Paul Seidel, Route 2, Roscoe, N.Y. 12776

Lewis-Wadhams School — boarding, ages 6 to 18. Herb Snitzer, Lewis-Wadhams School, R.D. Westport, N.Y. 12993

Minnesota Summerhill Community School — boarding, ages 6 to 17. Cortland Smith, Minnesota Summerhill Community School, Box 271, Spray Island, Spring Park, Minn. 55384

Modern Play School and Play Mountain Place — day, nursery and elementary. Phyllis Fleishman, 6063 Hargis St., Los Angeles, Cal. 94334.

Santa Fe Community School — Marie Kinney, P.O. Box 2241, Santa Fe, N.M. 87501